What is Snot?

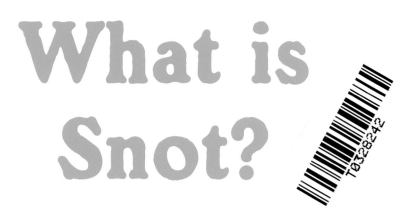

Contents

Written by Isabel Thomas

Collins

Your body is amazing, from head to toe.

Some things our bodies do can seem puzzling.

Let's solve these!

What is snot?

When you have a sniffle, slimy snot drips from your nose.

Snot is one of your body's **defences**! It traps **germs** and carries them away.

Why are shoulders so wide?

Shoulders are some of the largest **joints** in your body.

Most joints just bend back and forth.
Shoulders let arms **rotate** in a circle!

7

Where is my funny bone?

In your elbow! Bumping it can feel odd.

This bone touches a **nerve** inside your arm.
That's why it tingles when you bump it.

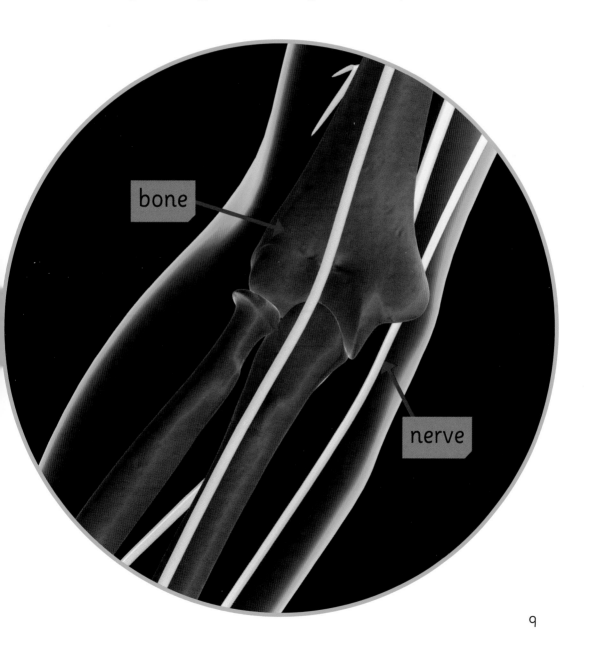

bone

nerve

How long could nails grow?

Fingernails and toenails grow too slowly
to notice.

But they never stop growing. If you didn't cut
your nails, they could grow longer than
your body!

Why do tummies rumble?

Your tummy rumbles when you are hungry.

The grumbly sound is gas inside your tummy.
It's your body's way of telling you to eat!

What are belly buttons for?

When you were an unborn baby, a tube carried food from your mother into your tummy.

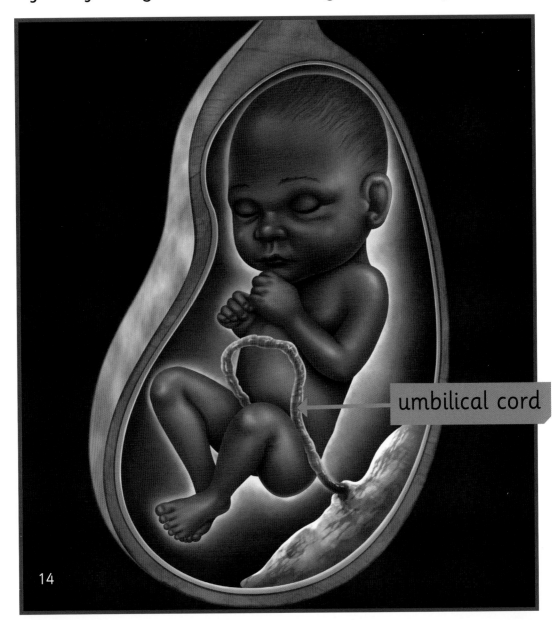

umbilical cord

When you were born, the tube dropped off.
Your belly button was left behind!

What are toes for?

Toes help you balance. You can spread them out when you exercise.

Why are toes ticklish?

When someone touches your feet,
the skin tingles.

Nerves in your skin send signals to your brain.
The signals arrive at two parts of your brain.

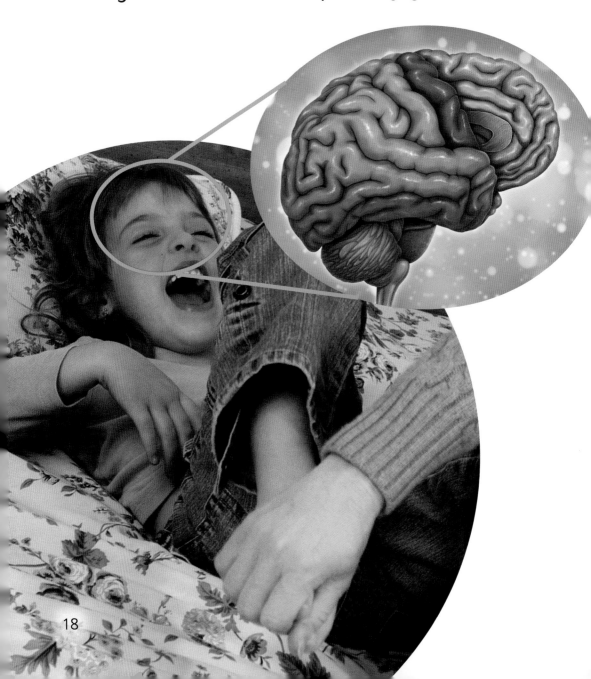

Both parts tell you what is happening.
This gives you the odd feeling called a tickle!

Glossary

defences how the body resists attacks from germs

germs tiny living things or viruses that can do us harm

joints places where two bones meet

nerve part of our body that carries signals to and from our brain

rotate turn around

Index

Your amazing body

❖ Review: After reading ❖

Use your assessment from hearing the children read to choose any GPCs, words or tricky words that need additional practice.

Read 1: Decoding

- Ask the children to explain the meaning of the following by offering a word or phrase of a similar meaning:
  Page 10: **notice** (e.g. *be aware of, spot*) Page 15: **button** (e.g. *mark left from tube*)
  Page 18: **signals** (e.g. *messages, signs*)

- Focus on words with the three spellings for the sounds /oa/ and /u/. Ask the children to read these words:
  toenails   some   shoulders   touches   elbow   mother   slowly   button

- Encourage the children to take turns to read a sentence without sounding out.
  Say: Try to blend in your head as you read.

Read 2: Prosody

- Turn to pages 4 and 5, and ask the children to read the pages, but to think about punctuation first. On page 4:
  - point out the question mark. Ask: Which words do we emphasise to show it is a question?
  - point out the comma. Say: Don't forget to pause here to separate the parts of the sentence.

- Let the children read both pages – do they read the exclamation on page 5 with an expression of surprise?

Read 3: Comprehension

- Look at the Contents together and ask: Which question did you think was the most interesting? Why? Which answer surprised you most? Why?
- Look together at the back cover blurb. Ask the children: Has the book solved some puzzles? What is the main subject of all these puzzles and answers? (*parts of the human body*)
- Hold a group quiz to encourage the children to skim and scan for information. Remind them to use the Contents and Index to find page numbers. Ask:
  - What page mentions mothers and babies? (*page 14*)
  - What makes the sound of a rumbling stomach? (*page 13: gas*)
  - Can you find me a definition of **germs**? (*page 20, glossary definition*)
- Turn to pages 22 and 23. Can the children remember an amazing fact that goes with each picture? Encourage them to look back in the book if necessary.